MW00338692

CONTENTS

HORSE INFORMATION — 3

CONTACT SHEETS — 25

BOOKKEEPING AND MAINTENANCE RECORDS — 33
Monthly Farm Expense Worksheets — 34
Farm Maintenance and Equipment Repair Records — 48

HORSE HEALTH — 51
Signs of Good Health — 53
Things to Look Out For — 53

ROUTINE CARE — 55
Vaccinations — 56
Worming — 61
Dental Work — 66
Feed Changes — 71
Supplement Changes — 76
Medicine Changes — 81
Turnout Changes — 86
Shoeing Changes — 91
Saddle Fit — 96
Chiropractic Work — 101
Massage Work — 106
Joint Injections — 111
Other Maintenance — 116
Lameness History — 122
Record of Farrier Visits — 142
Record of Vet Visits — 162

RECORDS — 183
Show Checklist — 185
Show Logs — 186
Race Records — 206
Mare Breeding Records — 226

WEEKLY PLANNER — 239

NOTES — 293

HORSE INFORMATION

"No philosophers so thoroughly
comprehend us as dogs and horses."
HERMAN MELVILLE

Name				
Age	Height	Sex	Weight	Date of Ownership

Breed	Breed Registration Number

Colour and Markings	Temperature	Pulse	Respiration Rate

Veterinarian Name and Contact Information

Farrier Name and Contact Information

Trainer Name and Contact Information

Hay (lbs or Flakes Per Day)	Feed Type and Amount Per Day
Supplement Type(s) and Amount(s) Per Day	Medications(s) and Amount(s) Per Day
Turnout Schedule	Notes

Name				
Age	Height	Sex	Weight	Date of Ownership

Breed	Breed Registration Number

Colour and Markings	Temperature	Pulse	Respiration Rate

Veterinarian Name and Contact Information

Farrier Name and Contact Information

Trainer Name and Contact Information

Hay (lbs or Flakes Per Day)	Feed Type and Amount Per Day

Supplement Type(s) and Amount(s) Per Day	Medications(s) and Amount(s) Per Day

Turnout Schedule	Notes

Name				
Age	Height	Sex	Weight	Date of Ownership

Breed	Breed Registration Number

Colour and Markings	Temperature	Pulse	Respiration Rate

Veterinarian Name and Contact Information

Farrier Name and Contact Information

Trainer Name and Contact Information

Hay (lbs or Flakes Per Day)	Feed Type and Amount Per Day

Supplement Type(s) and Amount(s) Per Day	Medications(s) and Amount(s) Per Day

Turnout Schedule	Notes

Name				
Age	Height	Sex	Weight	Date of Ownership
Breed			Breed Registration Number	
Colour and Markings		Temperature	Pulse	Respiration Rate

Veterinarian Name and Contact Information

Farrier Name and Contact Information

Trainer Name and Contact Information

Hay (lbs or Flakes Per Day)	Feed Type and Amount Per Day
Supplement Type(s) and Amount(s) Per Day	Medications(s) and Amount(s) Per Day
Turnout Schedule	Notes

Name				
Age	Height	Sex	Weight	Date of Ownership
Breed			Breed Registration Number	
Colour and Markings		Temperature	Pulse	Respiration Rate
Veterinarian Name and Contact Information				
Farrier Name and Contact Information				
Trainer Name and Contact Information				
Hay (lbs or Flakes Per Day)			Feed Type and Amount Per Day	
Supplement Type(s) and Amount(s) Per Day			Medications(s) and Amount(s) Per Day	
Turnout Schedule			Notes	

Name				
Age	Height	Sex	Weight	Date of Ownership
Breed			Breed Registration Number	
Colour and Markings		Temperature	Pulse	Respiration Rate

Veterinarian Name and Contact Information

Farrier Name and Contact Information

Trainer Name and Contact Information

Hay (lbs or Flakes Per Day)	Feed Type and Amount Per Day
Supplement Type(s) and Amount(s) Per Day	Medications(s) and Amount(s) Per Day
Turnout Schedule	Notes

Name				
Age	Height	Sex	Weight	Date of Ownership
Breed			Breed Registration Number	
Colour and Markings		Temperature	Pulse	Respiration Rate
Veterinarian Name and Contact Information				
Farrier Name and Contact Information				
Trainer Name and Contact Information				
Hay (lbs or Flakes Per Day)			Feed Type and Amount Per Day	
Supplement Type(s) and Amount(s) Per Day			Medications(s) and Amount(s) Per Day	
Turnout Schedule			Notes	

Name				
Age	**Height**	**Sex**	**Weight**	**Date of Ownership**
Breed			**Breed Registration Number**	
Colour and Markings		**Temperature**	**Pulse**	**Respiration Rate**
Veterinarian Name and Contact Information				
Farrier Name and Contact Information				
Trainer Name and Contact Information				
Hay (lbs or Flakes Per Day)		**Feed Type and Amount Per Day**		
Supplement Type(s) and Amount(s) Per Day		**Medications(s) and Amount(s) Per Day**		
Turnout Schedule		**Notes**		

Name				
Age	Height	Sex	Weight	Date of Ownership
Breed			Breed Registration Number	
Colour and Markings		Temperature	Pulse	Respiration Rate
Veterinarian Name and Contact Information				
Farrier Name and Contact Information				
Trainer Name and Contact Information				
Hay (lbs or Flakes Per Day)		Feed Type and Amount Per Day		
Supplement Type(s) and Amount(s) Per Day		Medications(s) and Amount(s) Per Day		
Turnout Schedule		Notes		

Name				

Age	Height	Sex	Weight	Date of Ownership

Breed		Breed Registration Number	

Colour and Markings	Temperature	Pulse	Respiration Rate

Veterinarian Name and Contact Information

Farrier Name and Contact Information

Trainer Name and Contact Information

Hay (lbs or Flakes Per Day)	Feed Type and Amount Per Day

Supplement Type(s) and Amount(s) Per Day	Medications(s) and Amount(s) Per Day

Turnout Schedule	Notes

Name				
Age	**Height**	**Sex**	**Weight**	**Date of Ownership**

Breed	Breed Registration Number

Colour and Markings		Temperature	Pulse	Respiration Rate

Veterinarian Name and Contact Information

Farrier Name and Contact Information

Trainer Name and Contact Information

Hay (lbs or Flakes Per Day)	Feed Type and Amount Per Day

Supplement Type(s) and Amount(s) Per Day	Medications(s) and Amount(s) Per Day

Turnout Schedule	Notes

Name				
Age	**Height**	**Sex**	**Weight**	**Date of Ownership**

Breed	Breed Registration Number

Colour and Markings	Temperature	Pulse	Respiration Rate

Veterinarian Name and Contact Information

Farrier Name and Contact Information

Trainer Name and Contact Information

Hay (lbs or Flakes Per Day)	Feed Type and Amount Per Day

Supplement Type(s) and Amount(s) Per Day	Medications(s) and Amount(s) Per Day

Turnout Schedule	Notes

Name				
Age	Height	Sex	Weight	Date of Ownership
Breed			Breed Registration Number	
Colour and Markings		Temperature	Pulse	Respiration Rate
Veterinarian Name and Contact Information				
Farrier Name and Contact Information				
Trainer Name and Contact Information				
Hay (lbs or Flakes Per Day)			Feed Type and Amount Per Day	
Supplement Type(s) and Amount(s) Per Day			Medications(s) and Amount(s) Per Day	
Turnout Schedule			Notes	

Name				
Age	Height	Sex	Weight	Date of Ownership
Breed			Breed Registration Number	
Colour and Markings		Temperature	Pulse	Respiration Rate
Veterinarian Name and Contact Information				
Farrier Name and Contact Information				
Trainer Name and Contact Information				
Hay (lbs or Flakes Per Day)		Feed Type and Amount Per Day		
Supplement Type(s) and Amount(s) Per Day		Medications(s) and Amount(s) Per Day		
Turnout Schedule		Notes		

Name				

Age	Height	Sex	Weight	Date of Ownership

Breed	Breed Registration Number

Colour and Markings	Temperature	Pulse	Respiration Rate

Veterinarian Name and Contact Information

Farrier Name and Contact Information

Trainer Name and Contact Information

Hay (lbs or Flakes Per Day)	Feed Type and Amount Per Day

Supplement Type(s) and Amount(s) Per Day	Medications(s) and Amount(s) Per Day

Turnout Schedule	Notes

Name				
Age	**Height**	**Sex**	**Weight**	**Date of Ownership**

Breed	Breed Registration Number

Colour and Markings	Temperature	Pulse	Respiration Rate

Veterinarian Name and Contact Information

Farrier Name and Contact Information

Trainer Name and Contact Information

Hay (lbs or Flakes Per Day)	Feed Type and Amount Per Day

Supplement Type(s) and Amount(s) Per Day	Medications(s) and Amount(s) Per Day

Turnout Schedule	Notes

Name				

Age	Height	Sex	Weight	Date of Ownership

Breed	Breed Registration Number

Colour and Markings	Temperature	Pulse	Respiration Rate

Veterinarian Name and Contact Information

Farrier Name and Contact Information

Trainer Name and Contact Information

Hay (lbs or Flakes Per Day)	Feed Type and Amount Per Day

Supplement Type(s) and Amount(s) Per Day	Medications(s) and Amount(s) Per Day

Turnout Schedule	Notes

Name				
Age	**Height**	**Sex**	**Weight**	**Date of Ownership**

Breed	Breed Registration Number

Colour and Markings	Temperature	Pulse	Respiration Rate

Veterinarian Name and Contact Information

Farrier Name and Contact Information

Trainer Name and Contact Information

Hay (lbs or Flakes Per Day)	Feed Type and Amount Per Day

Supplement Type(s) and Amount(s) Per Day	Medications(s) and Amount(s) Per Day

Turnout Schedule	Notes

Name				
Age	Height	Sex	Weight	Date of Ownership
Breed			Breed Registration Number	
Colour and Markings		Temperature	Pulse	Respiration Rate
Veterinarian Name and Contact Information				
Farrier Name and Contact Information				
Trainer Name and Contact Information				
Hay (lbs or Flakes Per Day)			Feed Type and Amount Per Day	
Supplement Type(s) and Amount(s) Per Day			Medications(s) and Amount(s) Per Day	
Turnout Schedule			Notes	

Name				
Age	**Height**	**Sex**	**Weight**	**Date of Ownership**
Breed			**Breed Registration Number**	
Colour and Markings		**Temperature**	**Pulse**	**Respiration Rate**

Veterinarian Name and Contact Information

Farrier Name and Contact Information

Trainer Name and Contact Information

Hay (lbs or Flakes Per Day)	Feed Type and Amount Per Day
Supplement Type(s) and Amount(s) Per Day	**Medications(s) and Amount(s) Per Day**
Turnout Schedule	**Notes**

CONTACTS

"If anybody expects to calm a horse down by
tiring him out with riding swiftly and far, his
supposition is the reverse of the truth."
XENOPHON

NAME	ADDRESS	EMAIL	PHONE
NAME	ADDRESS	EMAIL	PHONE

NAME	ADDRESS	EMAIL	PHONE
NAME	ADDRESS	EMAIL	PHONE

NAME	ADDRESS	EMAIL	PHONE

NAME	ADDRESS	EMAIL	PHONE
NAME	ADDRESS	EMAIL	PHONE

NAME	ADDRESS	EMAIL	PHONE
NAME	ADDRESS	EMAIL	PHONE

NAME	ADDRESS	EMAIL	PHONE
NAME	ADDRESS	EMAIL	PHONE

BOOKKEEPING AND MAINTENANCE RECORDS

"A horse loves freedom, and the weariest old work
horse will roll on the ground or break into a lumbering
gallop when he is turned loose into the open."
GERALD RAFERTY

Monthly Farm Expense Worksheets

Month: _____

CASH INCOME		FARM EXPENSES	
Board		Mortgage/Rent Payment	
Horse Sales		Property Taxes	
Training Fees		Insurance	
Lessons		Utilities	
Lease Fees		Property Repairs/ Maintenance	
Stud Fees		Equipment Repairs/ Maintenance	
Purse Money		Fuel/Gas/Oil	
Prize Money		Labour	
Other Income		Hay	
TOTAL INCOME		Feed	
		Medication/Supplements	
		Veterinary Services	
		Farrier Services	
		Training Fees	
		Breeding Fees	
		Entry Fees	
		Other Expenses	
		TOTAL EXPENSES	
NET INCOME			

NOTES:

Monthly Farm Expense Worksheets

Month: _____

CASH INCOME		FARM EXPENSES	
Board		Mortgage/Rent Payment	
Horse Sales		Property Taxes	
Training Fees		Insurance	
Lessons		Utilities	
Lease Fees		Property Repairs/ Maintenance	
Stud Fees		Equipment Repairs/ Maintenance	
Purse Money		Fuel/Gas/Oil	
Prize Money		Labour	
Other Income		Hay	
TOTAL INCOME		Feed	
		Medication/Supplements	
		Veterinary Services	
		Farrier Services	
		Training Fees	
		Breeding Fees	
		Entry Fees	
		Other Expenses	
		TOTAL EXPENSES	
NET INCOME			

NOTES:

Monthly Farm Expense Worksheets

Month: _____

CASH INCOME		FARM EXPENSES	
Board		Mortgage/Rent Payment	
Horse Sales		Property Taxes	
Training Fees		Insurance	
Lessons		Utilities	
Lease Fees		Property Repairs/ Maintenance	
Stud Fees		Equipment Repairs/ Maintenance	
Purse Money		Fuel/Gas/Oil	
Prize Money		Labour	
Other Income		Hay	
TOTAL INCOME		Feed	
		Medication/Supplements	
		Veterinary Services	
		Farrier Services	
		Training Fees	
		Breeding Fees	
		Entry Fees	
		Other Expenses	
		TOTAL EXPENSES	
NET INCOME			

NOTES:

Monthly Farm Expense Worksheets

Month: _____

CASH INCOME		FARM EXPENSES	
Board		Mortgage/Rent Payment	
Horse Sales		Property Taxes	
Training Fees		Insurance	
Lessons		Utilities	
Lease Fees		Property Repairs/ Maintenance	
Stud Fees		Equipment Repairs/ Maintenance	
Purse Money		Fuel/Gas/Oil	
Prize Money		Labour	
Other Income		Hay	
TOTAL INCOME		Feed	
		Medication/Supplements	
		Veterinary Services	
		Farrier Services	
		Training Fees	
		Breeding Fees	
		Entry Fees	
		Other Expenses	
		TOTAL EXPENSES	
NET INCOME			

NOTES:

Monthly Farm Expense Worksheets

Month: _____

CASH INCOME		FARM EXPENSES	
Board		Mortgage/Rent Payment	
Horse Sales		Property Taxes	
Training Fees		Insurance	
Lessons		Utilities	
Lease Fees		Property Repairs/ Maintenance	
Stud Fees		Equipment Repairs/ Maintenance	
Purse Money		Fuel/Gas/Oil	
Prize Money		Labour	
Other Income		Hay	
TOTAL INCOME		Feed	
		Medication/Supplements	
		Veterinary Services	
		Farrier Services	
		Training Fees	
		Breeding Fees	
		Entry Fees	
		Other Expenses	
		TOTAL EXPENSES	
NET INCOME			

NOTES:

Monthly Farm Expense Worksheets

Month: _____

CASH INCOME		FARM EXPENSES	
Board		Mortgage/Rent Payment	
Horse Sales		Property Taxes	
Training Fees		Insurance	
Lessons		Utilities	
Lease Fees		Property Repairs/ Maintenance	
Stud Fees		Equipment Repairs/ Maintenance	
Purse Money		Fuel/Gas/Oil	
Prize Money		Labour	
Other Income		Hay	
TOTAL INCOME		Feed	
		Medication/Supple-ments	
		Veterinary Services	
		Farrier Services	
		Training Fees	
		Breeding Fees	
		Entry Fees	
		Other Expenses	
		TOTAL EXPENSES	
NET INCOME			

NOTES:

Monthly Farm Expense Worksheets

Month: _____

CASH INCOME		FARM EXPENSES	
Board		Mortgage/Rent Payment	
Horse Sales		Property Taxes	
Training Fees		Insurance	
Lessons		Utilities	
Lease Fees		Property Repairs/ Maintenance	
Stud Fees		Equipment Repairs/ Maintenance	
Purse Money		Fuel/Gas/Oil	
Prize Money		Labour	
Other Income		Hay	
TOTAL INCOME		Feed	
		Medication/Supplements	
		Veterinary Services	
		Farrier Services	
		Training Fees	
		Breeding Fees	
		Entry Fees	
		Other Expenses	
		TOTAL EXPENSES	
NET INCOME			

NOTES:

40

Monthly Farm Expense Worksheets

Month: _____

CASH INCOME		FARM EXPENSES	
Board		Mortgage/Rent Payment	
Horse Sales		Property Taxes	
Training Fees		Insurance	
Lessons		Utilities	
Lease Fees		Property Repairs/ Maintenance	
Stud Fees		Equipment Repairs/ Maintenance	
Purse Money		Fuel/Gas/Oil	
Prize Money		Labour	
Other Income		Hay	
TOTAL INCOME		Feed	
		Medication/Supplements	
		Veterinary Services	
		Farrier Services	
		Training Fees	
		Breeding Fees	
		Entry Fees	
		Other Expenses	
		TOTAL EXPENSES	
NET INCOME			

NOTES:

Monthly Farm Expense Worksheets

Month: _____

CASH INCOME		FARM EXPENSES	
Board		Mortgage/Rent Payment	
Horse Sales		Property Taxes	
Training Fees		Insurance	
Lessons		Utilities	
Lease Fees		Property Repairs/ Maintenance	
Stud Fees		Equipment Repairs/ Maintenance	
Purse Money		Fuel/Gas/Oil	
Prize Money		Labour	
Other Income		Hay	
TOTAL INCOME		Feed	
		Medication/Supplements	
		Veterinary Services	
		Farrier Services	
		Training Fees	
		Breeding Fees	
		Entry Fees	
		Other Expenses	
		TOTAL EXPENSES	
NET INCOME			

NOTES:

Monthly Farm Expense Worksheets

Month: _____

CASH INCOME		FARM EXPENSES	
Board		Mortgage/Rent Payment	
Horse Sales		Property Taxes	
Training Fees		Insurance	
Lessons		Utilities	
Lease Fees		Property Repairs/ Maintenance	
Stud Fees		Equipment Repairs/ Maintenance	
Purse Money		Fuel/Gas/Oil	
Prize Money		Labour	
Other Income		Hay	
TOTAL INCOME		Feed	
		Medication/Supple-ments	
		Veterinary Services	
		Farrier Services	
		Training Fees	
		Breeding Fees	
		Entry Fees	
		Other Expenses	
		TOTAL EXPENSES	
NET INCOME			

NOTES:

Monthly Farm Expense Worksheets

Month: _____

CASH INCOME			FARM EXPENSES	
Board			Mortgage/Rent Payment	
Horse Sales			Property Taxes	
Training Fees			Insurance	
Lessons			Utilities	
Lease Fees			Property Repairs/ Maintenance	
Stud Fees			Equipment Repairs/ Maintenance	
Purse Money			Fuel/Gas/Oil	
Prize Money			Labour	
Other Income			Hay	
TOTAL INCOME			Feed	
			Medication/Supplements	
			Veterinary Services	
			Farrier Services	
			Training Fees	
			Breeding Fees	
			Entry Fees	
			Other Expenses	
			TOTAL EXPENSES	
NET INCOME				

NOTES:

Monthly Farm Expense Worksheets

Month: _____

CASH INCOME		FARM EXPENSES	
Board		Mortgage/Rent Payment	
Horse Sales		Property Taxes	
Training Fees		Insurance	
Lessons		Utilities	
Lease Fees		Property Repairs/ Maintenance	
Stud Fees		Equipment Repairs/ Maintenance	
Purse Money		Fuel/Gas/Oil	
Prize Money		Labour	
Other Income		Hay	
TOTAL INCOME		Feed	
		Medication/Supplements	
		Veterinary Services	
		Farrier Services	
		Training Fees	
		Breeding Fees	
		Entry Fees	
		Other Expenses	
		TOTAL EXPENSES	
NET INCOME			

NOTES:

Monthly Farm Expense Worksheets

Month: _____

CASH INCOME		FARM EXPENSES	
Board		Mortgage/Rent Payment	
Horse Sales		Property Taxes	
Training Fees		Insurance	
Lessons		Utilities	
Lease Fees		Property Repairs/ Maintenance	
Stud Fees		Equipment Repairs/ Maintenance	
Purse Money		Fuel/Gas/Oil	
Prize Money		Labour	
Other Income		Hay	
TOTAL INCOME		Feed	
		Medication/Supplements	
		Veterinary Services	
		Farrier Services	
		Training Fees	
		Breeding Fees	
		Entry Fees	
		Other Expenses	
		TOTAL EXPENSES	
NET INCOME			

NOTES:

Monthly Farm Expense Worksheets

Month: _____

CASH INCOME		FARM EXPENSES	
Board		Mortgage/Rent Payment	
Horse Sales		Property Taxes	
Training Fees		Insurance	
Lessons		Utilities	
Lease Fees		Property Repairs/ Maintenance	
Stud Fees		Equipment Repairs/ Maintenance	
Purse Money		Fuel/Gas/Oil	
Prize Money		Labour	
Other Income		Hay	
TOTAL INCOME		Feed	
		Medication/Supplements	
		Veterinary Services	
		Farrier Services	
		Training Fees	
		Breeding Fees	
		Entry Fees	
		Other Expenses	
		TOTAL EXPENSES	
NET INCOME			

NOTES:

Farm Maintenance and Equipment Repair Record

DATE	ISSUE	WORK DONE	REPAIR PERSON	COST

Farm Maintenance and Equipment Repair Record

DATE	ISSUE	WORK DONE	REPAIR PERSON	COST

Farm Maintenance and Equipment Repair Record

DATE	ISSUE	WORK DONE	REPAIR PERSON	COST

HORSE HEALTH

"If anybody expects to calm a horse down by
tiring him out with riding swiftly and far, his
supposition is the reverse of the truth."
XENOPHON

Signs of Good Health

An average horse at rest will have the following vital signs (individual horses will vary, so it's important to check what's normal for your horse):

Temperature: Approximately 38°C
Pulse: Between 28 and 40 Beats per Minute
Respiration: Between 8 to 16 Breaths per Minute

Other signs of good health include:

☐ Clear and Regular Heartbeat	☐ Soft, Smooth and Shiny Coat
☐ Quiet and Regular Breaths, Especially at Rest	☐ Good Appetite
☐ Clear, Alert Eyes	☐ Light and Regular Gut Sounds
☐ Relaxed Ears	☐ Firm Droppings
☐ Clean Nose (a little clear discharge is normal)	☐ Legs Free of Heat, Pain and Swelling
☐ Moist, Pink Gums	☐ Elastic Skin
☐ Quick Capillary Refill Time (less than 2 seconds if the gums are pressed with a thumb)	☐ Adequate Water Consumption (25-55 Liters of Water/Day)
☐ Willingness to Move Forward in Hand and Under Saddle	☐ Good Body Condition (a general rule for optimal body condition is to be able to feel the horse's ribs, but not see them)

Things To Look Out For

The following conditions may indicate a health or lameness issue, especially if they come on suddenly:

☐ Unusual or Extreme Mood Changes	☐ Discomfort While Eating, Spilling Food
☐ Lethargy, Disinterest	☐ Reluctance to Drink
☐ Shallow, Quick, Irregular or Laboured Breathing	☐ Dry, Pale Gums
☐ Rapid, Shallow Heartbeat	☐ Swollen Lymph Nodes
☐ Fever	☐ Thick Nasal Discharge
☐ Slow Capillary Refill Time (more than 2 seconds if the gums are pressed with a thumb)	☐ Cloudy, Congested, Runny, Squinting, Painful, Sunken or Swollen Eyes
☐ Changes in Appetite	☐ Sudden Changes in Body Condition
☐ Discomfort and Distress (can include excessive pawing, rolling, kicking out, elevated respiration rate)	☐ Dehydration (skin doesn't immediately spring back if gently pulled)
☐ Dull, Dry Flaky Coat	☐ Any Unusual or Sudden Swellings
☐ Discoloured Urine or Difficulty Urinating	☐ Heat, Pain or Swelling of Any Part of a Limb
☐ Loose Droppings or Difficulty Passing Droppings	☐ Unusual Reluctance to Move Forward
☐ Stiffness or Short-Strideness	☐ Reluctance to Perform Regular Tasks
☐ Long, Brittle, Cracked or Crumbling Hooves	

"A canter is a cure for every evil."
BENJAMIN DISRAELI

ROUTINE CARE

"Care, and not fine stables, makes a good horse."
DANISH PROVERB

Vaccinations

HORSE NAME	DATES	DESCRIPTION

Vaccinations

HORSE NAME	DATES	DESCRIPTION

Vaccinations

HORSE NAME	DATES	DESCRIPTION

Vaccinations

HORSE NAME	DATES	DESCRIPTION

Vaccinations

HORSE NAME	DATES	DESCRIPTION

Worming

HORSE NAME	DATES	DESCRIPTION

Worming

HORSE NAME	DATES	DESCRIPTION

Worming

HORSE NAME	DATES	DESCRIPTION

Worming

HORSE NAME	DATES	DESCRIPTION

Worming

HORSE NAME	DATES	DESCRIPTION

Dental Work

HORSE NAME	DATES	DESCRIPTION

Dental Work

HORSE NAME	DATES	DESCRIPTION

Dental Work

HORSE NAME	DATES	DESCRIPTION

Dental Work

HORSE NAME	DATES	DESCRIPTION

Dental Work

HORSE NAME	DATES	DESCRIPTION

Feed Changes

HORSE NAME	DATES	DESCRIPTION

Feed Changes

HORSE NAME	DATES	DESCRIPTION

Feed Changes

HORSE NAME	DATES	DESCRIPTION

Feed Changes

HORSE NAME	DATES	DESCRIPTION

Feed Changes

HORSE NAME	DATES	DESCRIPTION

Supplement Changes

HORSE NAME	DATES	DESCRIPTION

Supplement Changes

HORSE NAME	DATES	DESCRIPTION

Supplement Changes

HORSE NAME	DATES	DESCRIPTION

Supplement Changes

HORSE NAME	DATES	DESCRIPTION

Supplement Changes

HORSE NAME	DATES	DESCRIPTION

Medicine Changes

HORSE NAME	DATES	DESCRIPTION

Medicine Changes

HORSE NAME	DATES	DESCRIPTION

Medicine Changes

HORSE NAME	DATES	DESCRIPTION

Medicine Changes

HORSE NAME	DATES	DESCRIPTION

Medicine Changes

HORSE NAME	DATES	DESCRIPTION

Turnout Changes

HORSE NAME	DATES	DESCRIPTION

Turnout Changes

HORSE NAME	DATES	DESCRIPTION

Turnout Changes

HORSE NAME	DATES	DESCRIPTION

Turnout Changes

HORSE NAME	DATES	DESCRIPTION

Turnout Changes

HORSE NAME	DATES	DESCRIPTION

Shoeing Changes

HORSE NAME	DATES	DESCRIPTION

Shoeing Changes

HORSE NAME	DATES	DESCRIPTION

Shoeing Changes

HORSE NAME	DATES	DESCRIPTION

Shoeing Changes

HORSE NAME	DATES	DESCRIPTION

Shoeing Changes

HORSE NAME	DATES	DESCRIPTION

Saddle Fit

HORSE NAME	DATES	DESCRIPTION

Saddle Fit

HORSE NAME	DATES	DESCRIPTION

Saddle Fit

HORSE NAME	DATES	DESCRIPTION

Saddle Fit

HORSE NAME	DATES	DESCRIPTION

Saddle Fit

HORSE NAME	DATES	DESCRIPTION

Chiropractic Work

HORSE NAME	DATES	DESCRIPTION

Chiropractic Work

HORSE NAME	DATES	DESCRIPTION

Chiropractic Work

HORSE NAME	DATES	DESCRIPTION

Chiropractic Work

HORSE NAME	DATES	DESCRIPTION

Chiropractic Work

HORSE NAME	DATES	DESCRIPTION

Massage Work

HORSE NAME	DATES	DESCRIPTION

Massage Work

HORSE NAME	DATES	DESCRIPTION

Massage Work

HORSE NAME	DATES	DESCRIPTION

Massage Work

HORSE NAME	DATES	DESCRIPTION

Massage Work

HORSE NAME	DATES	DESCRIPTION

Joint Injections

HORSE NAME	DATES	DESCRIPTION

Joint Injections

HORSE NAME	DATES	DESCRIPTION

Joint Injections

HORSE NAME	DATES	DESCRIPTION

Joint Injections

HORSE NAME	DATES	DESCRIPTION

Joint Injections

HORSE NAME	DATES	DESCRIPTION

Other Maintenance

HORSE NAME	DATES	DESCRIPTION

Other Maintenance

HORSE NAME	DATES	DESCRIPTION

Other Maintenance

HORSE NAME	DATES	DESCRIPTION

Other Maintenance

HORSE NAME	DATES	DESCRIPTION

Other Maintenance

HORSE NAME	DATES	DESCRIPTION

Other Maintenance

HORSE NAME	DATES	DESCRIPTION

Lameness History

Horse Name: _____

DATE	DESCRIPTION	TREATMENT	OUTCOME

Lameness History

Horse Name: _____

DATE	DESCRIPTION	TREATMENT	OUTCOME

Lameness History

Horse Name: _____

DATE	DESCRIPTION	TREATMENT	OUTCOME

Lameness History

Horse Name: _____

DATE	DESCRIPTION	TREATMENT	OUTCOME

Lameness History

Horse Name: _____

DATE	DESCRIPTION	TREATMENT	OUTCOME

Lameness History

Horse Name: _____

DATE	DESCRIPTION	TREATMENT	OUTCOME

Lameness History

Horse Name: _____

DATE	DESCRIPTION	TREATMENT	OUTCOME

Lameness History

Horse Name: _____

DATE	DESCRIPTION	TREATMENT	OUTCOME

Lameness History

Horse Name: _____

DATE	DESCRIPTION	TREATMENT	OUTCOME

Lameness History

Horse Name: _____

DATE	DESCRIPTION	TREATMENT	OUTCOME

Lameness History

Horse Name: _____

DATE	DESCRIPTION	TREATMENT	OUTCOME

Lameness History

Horse Name: _____

DATE	DESCRIPTION	TREATMENT	OUTCOME

Lameness History

Horse Name: _____

DATE	DESCRIPTION	TREATMENT	OUTCOME

Lameness History

Horse Name: _____

DATE	DESCRIPTION	TREATMENT	OUTCOME

Lameness History

Horse Name: _____

DATE	DESCRIPTION	TREATMENT	OUTCOME

Lameness History

Horse Name: _____

DATE	DESCRIPTION	TREATMENT	OUTCOME

Lameness History

Horse Name: _____

DATE	DESCRIPTION	TREATMENT	OUTCOME

Lameness History

Horse Name: _____

DATE	DESCRIPTION	TREATMENT	OUTCOME

Lameness History

Horse Name: _____

DATE	DESCRIPTION	TREATMENT	OUTCOME

Lameness History

Horse Name: _____

DATE	DESCRIPTION	TREATMENT	OUTCOME

Record of Farrier Visits

Horse Name: _____

DATE	WORK DONE	NOTES / RECOMMENDATIONS

Record of Farrier Visits

Horse Name: _____

DATE	WORK DONE	NOTES / RECOMMENDATIONS

Record of Farrier Visits

Horse Name: _____

DATE	WORK DONE	NOTES / RECOMMENDATIONS

Record of Farrier Visits

Horse Name: _____

DATE	WORK DONE	NOTES / RECOMMENDATIONS

Record of Farrier Visits

Horse Name: _____

DATE	WORK DONE	NOTES / RECOMMENDATIONS

Record of Farrier Visits

Horse Name: _____

DATE	WORK DONE	NOTES / RECOMMENDATIONS

Record of Farrier Visits

Horse Name: _____

DATE	WORK DONE	NOTES / RECOMMENDATIONS

Record of Farrier Visits

Horse Name: _____

DATE	WORK DONE	NOTES / RECOMMENDATIONS

Record of Farrier Visits

Horse Name: _____

DATE	WORK DONE	NOTES / RECOMMENDATIONS

Record of Farrier Visits

Horse Name: _____

DATE	WORK DONE	NOTES / RECOMMENDATIONS

Record of Farrier Visits

Horse Name: _____

DATE	WORK DONE	NOTES / RECOMMENDATIONS

Record of Farrier Visits

Horse Name: _____

DATE	WORK DONE	NOTES / RECOMMENDATIONS

Record of Farrier Visits

Horse Name: _____

DATE	WORK DONE	NOTES / RECOMMENDATIONS

Record of Farrier Visits

Horse Name: _____

DATE	WORK DONE	NOTES / RECOMMENDATIONS

Record of Farrier Visits

Horse Name: _____

DATE	WORK DONE	NOTES / RECOMMENDATIONS

Record of Farrier Visits

Horse Name: _____

DATE	WORK DONE	NOTES / RECOMMENDATIONS

Record of Farrier Visits

Horse Name: _____

DATE	WORK DONE	NOTES / RECOMMENDATIONS

Record of Farrier Visits

Horse Name: _____

DATE	WORK DONE	NOTES / RECOMMENDATIONS

Record of Farrier Visits

Horse Name: _____

DATE	WORK DONE	NOTES / RECOMMENDATIONS

Record of Farrier Visits

Horse Name: _____

DATE	WORK DONE	NOTES / RECOMMENDATIONS

Record of Vet Visits

Horse Name: _____

DATE	WORK DONE	NOTES / RECOMMENDATIONS

Record of Vet Visits

Horse Name: _____

DATE	WORK DONE	NOTES / RECOMMENDATIONS

Record of Vet Visits

Horse Name: _____

DATE	WORK DONE	NOTES / RECOMMENDATIONS

Record of Vet Visits

Horse Name: _____

DATE	WORK DONE	NOTES / RECOMMENDATIONS

Record of Vet Visits

Horse Name: _____

DATE	WORK DONE	NOTES / RECOMMENDATIONS

Record of Vet Visits

Horse Name: _____

DATE	WORK DONE	NOTES / RECOMMENDATIONS

Record of Vet Visits

Horse Name: _____

DATE	WORK DONE	NOTES / RECOMMENDATIONS

Record of Vet Visits

Horse Name: _____

DATE	WORK DONE	NOTES / RECOMMENDATIONS

Record of Vet Visits

Horse Name: _____

DATE	WORK DONE	NOTES / RECOMMENDATIONS

Record of Vet Visits

Horse Name: _____

DATE	WORK DONE	NOTES / RECOMMENDATIONS

Record of Vet Visits

Horse Name: _____

DATE	WORK DONE	NOTES / RECOMMENDATIONS

Record of Vet Visits

Horse Name: _____

DATE	WORK DONE	NOTES / RECOMMENDATIONS

Record of Vet Visits

Horse Name: _____

DATE	WORK DONE	NOTES / RECOMMENDATIONS

Record of Vet Visits

Horse Name: _____

DATE	WORK DONE	NOTES / RECOMMENDATIONS

Record of Vet Visits

Horse Name: _____

DATE	WORK DONE	NOTES / RECOMMENDATIONS

Record of Vet Visits

Horse Name: _____

DATE	WORK DONE	NOTES / RECOMMENDATIONS

Record of Vet Visits

Horse Name: _____

DATE	WORK DONE	NOTES / RECOMMENDATIONS

Record of Vet Visits

Horse Name: _____

DATE	WORK DONE	NOTES / RECOMMENDATIONS

Record of Vet Visits

Horse Name: _____

DATE	WORK DONE	NOTES / RECOMMENDATIONS

Record of Vet Visits

Horse Name: _____

DATE	WORK DONE	NOTES / RECOMMENDATIONS

RECORDS

"No hour of life is wasted
that is spent in the saddle."
WINSTON CHURCHILL

Show Checklist

FOR THE HORSE

☐ Equine First Aid Kit
☐ Hay and Hay Net
☐ Water Buckets, Clips and Jugs of Water
☐ Feed and Supplements
☐ Halter, Lead Rope, Lunge Line
☐ Back up Halter, Lead Rope, Lunge Line
☐ Tack and Back up Tack
☐ Tack Cleaning Supplies
☐ Wraps and Boots (regular and shipping)
☐ Cooler and/or Sheet
☐ Grooming Supplies and Towels
☐ Bath Supplies
☐ Fly Spray
☐ Braiding Kit and Scissors
☐ Lots of Treats

FOR THE RIDER

☐ Rider Health Card
☐ Human First Aid Kit
☐ Sunscreen and Sun Protection
☐ Water
☐ Helmet
☐ Show Clothes and Safety Vest
☐ Cover-up Clothes for Grooming
☐ Gloves
☐ Rain Gear
☐ Safety Pins, Sewing Kit, Spot Cleaner
☐ Folding Chairs
☐ Cell Phone and List of Emergency Numbers
☐ Watch

FOR THE TRAILER

☐ Safety Check
☐ Spare Tire and Jack
☐ Extra Ties
☐ Hay Nets and Hay
☐ Bedding
☐ Muck Bucket and Forks
☐ Duct Tape, Flashlight

FOR / FROM THE SHOW OFFICE

☐ Association Memberships
☐ Horse Passport
☐ Registration Papers
☐ Negative Coggins and/or Other Required Health Documentation
☐ Rulebook
☐ Cash or Chequebook
☐ Copy of Tests, Patterns and Class Lists

"Many people have sighed for the 'good old days' and regretted the 'passing of the horse,' but today, when only those who like horses own them, it is a far better time for horses."
C.W. ANDERSON

Show Log

Horse Name: _____

DATE	VENUE / SERIES	JUDGE	CLASS	PLACING	NUMBER IN CLASS	POINTS

Show Log

Horse Name: _____

DATE	VENUE / SERIES	JUDGE	CLASS	PLACING	NUMBER IN CLASS	POINTS

Show Log

Horse Name: _____

DATE	VENUE / SERIES	JUDGE	CLASS	PLACING	NUMBER IN CLASS	POINTS

Show Log

Horse Name: _____

DATE	VENUE / SERIES	JUDGE	CLASS	PLACING	NUMBER IN CLASS	POINTS

Show Log

Horse Name: _____

DATE	VENUE / SERIES	JUDGE	CLASS	PLACING	NUMBER IN CLASS	POINTS

Show Log

Horse Name: _____

DATE	VENUE / SERIES	JUDGE	CLASS	PLACING	NUMBER IN CLASS	POINTS

Show Log

Horse Name: _____

DATE	VENUE / SERIES	JUDGE	CLASS	PLACING	NUMBER IN CLASS	POINTS

Show Log

Horse Name: _____

DATE	VENUE / SERIES	JUDGE	CLASS	PLACING	NUMBER IN CLASS	POINTS

Show Log

Horse Name: _____

DATE	VENUE / SERIES	JUDGE	CLASS	PLACING	NUMBER IN CLASS	POINTS

Show Log

Horse Name: _____

DATE	VENUE / SERIES	JUDGE	CLASS	PLACING	NUMBER IN CLASS	POINTS

Show Log

Horse Name: _____

DATE	VENUE / SERIES	JUDGE	CLASS	PLACING	NUMBER IN CLASS	POINTS

Show Log

Horse Name: _____

DATE	VENUE / SERIES	JUDGE	CLASS	PLACING	NUMBER IN CLASS	POINTS

Show Log

Horse Name: _____

DATE	VENUE / SERIES	JUDGE	CLASS	PLACING	NUMBER IN CLASS	POINTS

Show Log

Horse Name: _____

DATE	VENUE / SERIES	JUDGE	CLASS	PLACING	NUMBER IN CLASS	POINTS

Show Log

Horse Name: _____

DATE	VENUE / SERIES	JUDGE	CLASS	PLACING	NUMBER IN CLASS	POINTS

Show Log

Horse Name: _____

DATE	VENUE / SERIES	JUDGE	CLASS	PLACING	NUMBER IN CLASS	POINTS

Show Log

Horse Name: _____

DATE	VENUE / SERIES	JUDGE	CLASS	PLACING	NUMBER IN CLASS	POINTS

Show Log

Horse Name: _____

DATE	VENUE / SERIES	JUDGE	CLASS	PLACING	NUMBER IN CLASS	POINTS

Show Log

Horse Name: _____

DATE	VENUE / SERIES	JUDGE	CLASS	PLACING	NUMBER IN CLASS	POINTS

Show Log

Horse Name: _____

DATE	VENUE / SERIES	JUDGE	CLASS	PLACING	NUMBER IN CLASS	POINTS

Race Records

Horse Name: _____

DATE	VENUE	RACE TYPE	PURSE	DISTANCE	PLACING	WINNINGS

Race Records

Horse Name: _____

DATE	VENUE	RACE TYPE	PURSE	DISTANCE	PLACING	WINNINGS

Race Records

Horse Name: _____

DATE	VENUE	RACE TYPE	PURSE	DISTANCE	PLACING	WINNINGS

Race Records

Horse Name: _____

DATE	VENUE	RACE TYPE	PURSE	DISTANCE	PLACING	WINNINGS

Race Records

Horse Name: _____

DATE	VENUE	RACE TYPE	PURSE	DISTANCE	PLACING	WINNINGS

Race Records

Horse Name: _____

DATE	VENUE	RACE TYPE	PURSE	DISTANCE	PLACING	WINNINGS

Race Records

Horse Name: _____

DATE	VENUE	RACE TYPE	PURSE	DISTANCE	PLACING	WINNINGS

Race Records

Horse Name: _____

DATE	VENUE	RACE TYPE	PURSE	DISTANCE	PLACING	WINNINGS

Race Records

Horse Name: _____

DATE	VENUE	RACE TYPE	PURSE	DISTANCE	PLACING	WINNINGS

Race Records

Horse Name: _____

DATE	VENUE	RACE TYPE	PURSE	DISTANCE	PLACING	WINNINGS

Race Records

Horse Name: _____

DATE	VENUE	RACE TYPE	PURSE	DISTANCE	PLACING	WINNINGS

Race Records

Horse Name: _____

DATE	VENUE	RACE TYPE	PURSE	DISTANCE	PLACING	WINNINGS

Race Records

Horse Name: _____

DATE	VENUE	RACE TYPE	PURSE	DISTANCE	PLACING	WINNINGS

Race Records

Horse Name: _____

DATE	VENUE	RACE TYPE	PURSE	DISTANCE	PLACING	WINNINGS

Race Records

Horse Name: _____

DATE	VENUE	RACE TYPE	PURSE	DISTANCE	PLACING	WINNINGS

Race Records

Horse Name: _____

DATE	VENUE	RACE TYPE	PURSE	DISTANCE	PLACING	WINNINGS

Race Records

Horse Name: _____

DATE	VENUE	RACE TYPE	PURSE	DISTANCE	PLACING	WINNINGS

Race Records

Horse Name: _____

DATE	VENUE	RACE TYPE	PURSE	DISTANCE	PLACING	WINNINGS

Race Records

Horse Name: _____

DATE	VENUE	RACE TYPE	PURSE	DISTANCE	PLACING	WINNINGS

Race Records

Horse Name: _____

DATE	VENUE	RACE TYPE	PURSE	DISTANCE	PLACING	WINNINGS

Mare Breeding Record

Horse's Name:	Registration #:
Breed:	Age:
Foal at Side: Y N	Maiden: Y N
Stallion Name:	Owned by:
Breeding Method: Pasture Hand AI	Semen: Fresh Frozen
Breeding History:	

Code: N – no signs of heat   X – in heat   T – teased   B – bred   C – pregnancy check
P – pregnant   A – aborted   V – veterinary exam

January	1	2	3	4	5	6	7	8	9	10	11	12	13	14	15	16
	17	18	19	20	21	22	23	24	25	26	27	28	29	30	31	
February	1	2	3	4	5	6	7	8	9	10	11	12	13	14	15	16
	17	18	19	20	21	22	23	24	25	26	27	28	29			
March	1	2	3	4	5	6	7	8	9	10	11	12	13	14	15	16
	17	18	19	20	21	22	23	24	25	26	27	28	29	30	31	
April	1	2	3	4	5	6	7	8	9	10	11	12	13	14	15	16
	17	18	19	20	21	22	23	24	25	26	27	28	29	30		
May	1	2	3	4	5	6	7	8	9	10	11	12	13	14	15	16
	17	18	19	20	21	22	23	24	25	26	27	28	29	30	31	
June	1	2	3	4	5	6	7	8	9	10	11	12	13	14	15	16
	17	18	19	20	21	22	23	24	25	26	27	28	29	30		
July	1	2	3	4	5	6	7	8	9	10	11	12	13	14	15	16
	17	18	19	20	21	22	23	24	25	26	27	28	29	30	31	
August	1	2	3	4	5	6	7	8	9	10	11	12	13	14	15	16
	17	18	19	20	21	22	23	24	25	26	27	28	29	30	31	

Notes:

Mare Breeding Record

Horse's Name:	Registration #:
Breed:	Age:
Foal at Side: Y N	Maiden: Y N
Stallion Name:	Owned by:
Breeding Method: Pasture Hand AI	Semen: Fresh Frozen

Breeding History:

Code: N – no signs of heat   X – in heat   T – teased   B – bred   C – pregnancy check
P – pregnant   A – aborted   V – veterinary exam

January	1	2	3	4	5	6	7	8	9	10	11	12	13	14	15	16
	17	18	19	20	21	22	23	24	25	26	27	28	29	30	31	
February	1	2	3	4	5	6	7	8	9	10	11	12	13	14	15	16
	17	18	19	20	21	22	23	24	25	26	27	28	29			
March	1	2	3	4	5	6	7	8	9	10	11	12	13	14	15	16
	17	18	19	20	21	22	23	24	25	26	27	28	29	30	31	
April	1	2	3	4	5	6	7	8	9	10	11	12	13	14	15	16
	17	18	19	20	21	22	23	24	25	26	27	28	29	30		
May	1	2	3	4	5	6	7	8	9	10	11	12	13	14	15	16
	17	18	19	20	21	22	23	24	25	26	27	28	29	30	31	
June	1	2	3	4	5	6	7	8	9	10	11	12	13	14	15	16
	17	18	19	20	21	22	23	24	25	26	27	28	29	30		
July	1	2	3	4	5	6	7	8	9	10	11	12	13	14	15	16
	17	18	19	20	21	22	23	24	25	26	27	28	29	30	31	
August	1	2	3	4	5	6	7	8	9	10	11	12	13	14	15	16
	17	18	19	20	21	22	23	24	25	26	27	28	29	30	31	

Notes:

Mare Breeding Record

Horse's Name:		Registration #:	
Breed:		Age:	
Foal at Side:	Y N	Maiden:	Y N
Stallion Name:		Owned by:	
Breeding Method:	Pasture Hand AI	Semen:	Fresh Frozen
Breeding History:			

Code: N – no signs of heat   X – in heat   T – teased   B – bred   C – pregnancy check
P – pregnant   A – aborted   V – veterinary exam

January	1	2	3	4	5	6	7	8	9	10	11	12	13	14	15	16
	17	18	19	20	21	22	23	24	25	26	27	28	29	30	31	
February	1	2	3	4	5	6	7	8	9	10	11	12	13	14	15	16
	17	18	19	20	21	22	23	24	25	26	27	28	29			
March	1	2	3	4	5	6	7	8	9	10	11	12	13	14	15	16
	17	18	19	20	21	22	23	24	25	26	27	28	29	30	31	
April	1	2	3	4	5	6	7	8	9	10	11	12	13	14	15	16
	17	18	19	20	21	22	23	24	25	26	27	28	29	30		
May	1	2	3	4	5	6	7	8	9	10	11	12	13	14	15	16
	17	18	19	20	21	22	23	24	25	26	27	28	29	30	31	
June	1	2	3	4	5	6	7	8	9	10	11	12	13	14	15	16
	17	18	19	20	21	22	23	24	25	26	27	28	29	30		
July	1	2	3	4	5	6	7	8	9	10	11	12	13	14	15	16
	17	18	19	20	21	22	23	24	25	26	27	28	29	30	31	
August	1	2	3	4	5	6	7	8	9	10	11	12	13	14	15	16
	17	18	19	20	21	22	23	24	25	26	27	28	29	30	31	

Notes:

Mare Breeding Record

Horse's Name:		Registration #:	
Breed:		**Age:**	
Foal at Side: Y N		**Maiden:** Y N	
Stallion Name:		**Owned by:**	
Breeding Method: Pasture Hand AI		**Semen:** Fresh Frozen	

Breeding History:

Code: N – no signs of heat   X – in heat   T – teased   B – bred   C – pregnancy check
P – pregnant   A – aborted   V – veterinary exam

	1	2	3	4	5	6	7	8	9	10	11	12	13	14	15	16
January	17	18	19	20	21	22	23	24	25	26	27	28	29	30	31	
February	1	2	3	4	5	6	7	8	9	10	11	12	13	14	15	16
	17	18	19	20	21	22	23	24	25	26	27	28	29			
March	1	2	3	4	5	6	7	8	9	10	11	12	13	14	15	16
	17	18	19	20	21	22	23	24	25	26	27	28	29	30	31	
April	1	2	3	4	5	6	7	8	9	10	11	12	13	14	15	16
	17	18	19	20	21	22	23	24	25	26	27	28	29	30		
May	1	2	3	4	5	6	7	8	9	10	11	12	13	14	15	16
	17	18	19	20	21	22	23	24	25	26	27	28	29	30	31	
June	1	2	3	4	5	6	7	8	9	10	11	12	13	14	15	16
	17	18	19	20	21	22	23	24	25	26	27	28	29	30		
July	1	2	3	4	5	6	7	8	9	10	11	12	13	14	15	16
	17	18	19	20	21	22	23	24	25	26	27	28	29	30	31	
August	1	2	3	4	5	6	7	8	9	10	11	12	13	14	15	16
	17	18	19	20	21	22	23	24	25	26	27	28	29	30	31	

Notes:

Mare Breeding Record

Horse's Name:								Registration #:							
Breed:								**Age:**							
Foal at Side: Y N								**Maiden:** Y N							
Stallion Name:								**Owned by:**							
Breeding Method: Pasture Hand AI								**Semen:** Fresh Frozen							

Breeding History:

Code: N – no signs of heat   X – in heat   T – teased   B – bred   C – pregnancy check
        P – pregnant   A – aborted   V – veterinary exam

January	1	2	3	4	5	6	7	8	9	10	11	12	13	14	15	16
	17	18	19	20	21	22	23	24	25	26	27	28	29	30	31	
February	1	2	3	4	5	6	7	8	9	10	11	12	13	14	15	16
	17	18	19	20	21	22	23	24	25	26	27	28	29			
March	1	2	3	4	5	6	7	8	9	10	11	12	13	14	15	16
	17	18	19	20	21	22	23	24	25	26	27	28	29	30	31	
April	1	2	3	4	5	6	7	8	9	10	11	12	13	14	15	16
	17	18	19	20	21	22	23	24	25	26	27	28	29	30		
May	1	2	3	4	5	6	7	8	9	10	11	12	13	14	15	16
	17	18	19	20	21	22	23	24	25	26	27	28	29	30	31	
June	1	2	3	4	5	6	7	8	9	10	11	12	13	14	15	16
	17	18	19	20	21	22	23	24	25	26	27	28	29	30		
July	1	2	3	4	5	6	7	8	9	10	11	12	13	14	15	16
	17	18	19	20	21	22	23	24	25	26	27	28	29	30	31	
August	1	2	3	4	5	6	7	8	9	10	11	12	13	14	15	16
	17	18	19	20	21	22	23	24	25	26	27	28	29	30	31	

Notes:

Mare Breeding Record

Horse's Name:		Registration #:	
Breed:		**Age:**	
Foal at Side: Y N		**Maiden:** Y N	
Stallion Name:		**Owned by:**	
Breeding Method: Pasture Hand AI		**Semen:** Fresh Frozen	
Breeding History:			

Code: N – no signs of heat   X – in heat   T – teased   B – bred   C – pregnancy check
P – pregnant   A – aborted   V – veterinary exam

January	1	2	3	4	5	6	7	8	9	10	11	12	13	14	15	16
	17	18	19	20	21	22	23	24	25	26	27	28	29	30	31	
February	1	2	3	4	5	6	7	8	9	10	11	12	13	14	15	16
	17	18	19	20	21	22	23	24	25	26	27	28	29			
March	1	2	3	4	5	6	7	8	9	10	11	12	13	14	15	16
	17	18	19	20	21	22	23	24	25	26	27	28	29	30	31	
April	1	2	3	4	5	6	7	8	9	10	11	12	13	14	15	16
	17	18	19	20	21	22	23	24	25	26	27	28	29	30		
May	1	2	3	4	5	6	7	8	9	10	11	12	13	14	15	16
	17	18	19	20	21	22	23	24	25	26	27	28	29	30	31	
June	1	2	3	4	5	6	7	8	9	10	11	12	13	14	15	16
	17	18	19	20	21	22	23	24	25	26	27	28	29	30		
July	1	2	3	4	5	6	7	8	9	10	11	12	13	14	15	16
	17	18	19	20	21	22	23	24	25	26	27	28	29	30	31	
August	1	2	3	4	5	6	7	8	9	10	11	12	13	14	15	16
	17	18	19	20	21	22	23	24	25	26	27	28	29	30	31	

Notes:

Mare Breeding Record

Horse's Name:	Registration #:
Breed:	Age:
Foal at Side: Y N	Maiden: Y N
Stallion Name:	Owned by:
Breeding Method: Pasture Hand AI	Semen: Fresh Frozen

Breeding History:

Code: N – no signs of heat   X – in heat   T – teased   B – bred   C – pregnancy check
P – pregnant   A – aborted   V – veterinary exam

January	1	2	3	4	5	6	7	8	9	10	11	12	13	14	15	16
	17	18	19	20	21	22	23	24	25	26	27	28	29	30	31	
February	1	2	3	4	5	6	7	8	9	10	11	12	13	14	15	16
	17	18	19	20	21	22	23	24	25	26	27	28	29			
March	1	2	3	4	5	6	7	8	9	10	11	12	13	14	15	16
	17	18	19	20	21	22	23	24	25	26	27	28	29	30	31	
April	1	2	3	4	5	6	7	8	9	10	11	12	13	14	15	16
	17	18	19	20	21	22	23	24	25	26	27	28	29	30		
May	1	2	3	4	5	6	7	8	9	10	11	12	13	14	15	16
	17	18	19	20	21	22	23	24	25	26	27	28	29	30	31	
June	1	2	3	4	5	6	7	8	9	10	11	12	13	14	15	16
	17	18	19	20	21	22	23	24	25	26	27	28	29	30		
July	1	2	3	4	5	6	7	8	9	10	11	12	13	14	15	16
	17	18	19	20	21	22	23	24	25	26	27	28	29	30	31	
August	1	2	3	4	5	6	7	8	9	10	11	12	13	14	15	16
	17	18	19	20	21	22	23	24	25	26	27	28	29	30	31	

Notes:

Mare Breeding Record

Horse's Name:	**Registration #:**
Breed:	**Age:**
Foal at Side: Y N	**Maiden:** Y N
Stallion Name:	**Owned by:**
Breeding Method: Pasture Hand AI	**Semen:** Fresh Frozen

Breeding History:

Code: N – no signs of heat   X – in heat   T – teased   B – bred   C – pregnancy check
       P – pregnant   A – aborted   V – veterinary exam

Month																
January	1	2	3	4	5	6	7	8	9	10	11	12	13	14	15	16
	17	18	19	20	21	22	23	24	25	26	27	28	29	30	31	
February	1	2	3	4	5	6	7	8	9	10	11	12	13	14	15	16
	17	18	19	20	21	22	23	24	25	26	27	28	29			
March	1	2	3	4	5	6	7	8	9	10	11	12	13	14	15	16
	17	18	19	20	21	22	23	24	25	26	27	28	29	30	31	
April	1	2	3	4	5	6	7	8	9	10	11	12	13	14	15	16
	17	18	19	20	21	22	23	24	25	26	27	28	29	30		
May	1	2	3	4	5	6	7	8	9	10	11	12	13	14	15	16
	17	18	19	20	21	22	23	24	25	26	27	28	29	30	31	
June	1	2	3	4	5	6	7	8	9	10	11	12	13	14	15	16
	17	18	19	20	21	22	23	24	25	26	27	28	29	30		
July	1	2	3	4	5	6	7	8	9	10	11	12	13	14	15	16
	17	18	19	20	21	22	23	24	25	26	27	28	29	30	31	
August	1	2	3	4	5	6	7	8	9	10	11	12	13	14	15	16
	17	18	19	20	21	22	23	24	25	26	27	28	29	30	31	

Notes:

Mare Breeding Record

Horse's Name:	**Registration #:**
Breed:	**Age:**
Foal at Side: Y N	**Maiden:** Y N
Stallion Name:	**Owned by:**
Breeding Method: Pasture Hand AI	**Semen:** Fresh Frozen
Breeding History:	

Code: N – no signs of heat   X – in heat   T – teased   B – bred   C – pregnancy check
P – pregnant   A – aborted   V – veterinary exam

January	1	2	3	4	5	6	7	8	9	10	11	12	13	14	15	16
	17	18	19	20	21	22	23	24	25	26	27	28	29	30	31	
February	1	2	3	4	5	6	7	8	9	10	11	12	13	14	15	16
	17	18	19	20	21	22	23	24	25	26	27	28	29			
March	1	2	3	4	5	6	7	8	9	10	11	12	13	14	15	16
	17	18	19	20	21	22	23	24	25	26	27	28	29	30	31	
April	1	2	3	4	5	6	7	8	9	10	11	12	13	14	15	16
	17	18	19	20	21	22	23	24	25	26	27	28	29	30		
May	1	2	3	4	5	6	7	8	9	10	11	12	13	14	15	16
	17	18	19	20	21	22	23	24	25	26	27	28	29	30	31	
June	1	2	3	4	5	6	7	8	9	10	11	12	13	14	15	16
	17	18	19	20	21	22	23	24	25	26	27	28	29	30		
July	1	2	3	4	5	6	7	8	9	10	11	12	13	14	15	16
	17	18	19	20	21	22	23	24	25	26	27	28	29	30	31	
August	1	2	3	4	5	6	7	8	9	10	11	12	13	14	15	16
	17	18	19	20	21	22	23	24	25	26	27	28	29	30	31	

Notes:

Mare Breeding Record

Horse's Name:		Registration #:	
Breed:		Age:	
Foal at Side: Y N		Maiden: Y N	
Stallion Name:		Owned by:	
Breeding Method: Pasture Hand AI		Semen: Fresh Frozen	

Breeding History:

Code: N – no signs of heat   X – in heat   T – teased   B – bred   C – pregnancy check
        P – pregnant   A – aborted   V – veterinary exam

Month																
January	1	2	3	4	5	6	7	8	9	10	11	12	13	14	15	16
	17	18	19	20	21	22	23	24	25	26	27	28	29	30	31	
February	1	2	3	4	5	6	7	8	9	10	11	12	13	14	15	16
	17	18	19	20	21	22	23	24	25	26	27	28	29			
March	1	2	3	4	5	6	7	8	9	10	11	12	13	14	15	16
	17	18	19	20	21	22	23	24	25	26	27	28	29	30	31	
April	1	2	3	4	5	6	7	8	9	10	11	12	13	14	15	16
	17	18	19	20	21	22	23	24	25	26	27	28	29	30		
May	1	2	3	4	5	6	7	8	9	10	11	12	13	14	15	16
	17	18	19	20	21	22	23	24	25	26	27	28	29	30	31	
June	1	2	3	4	5	6	7	8	9	10	11	12	13	14	15	16
	17	18	19	20	21	22	23	24	25	26	27	28	29	30		
July	1	2	3	4	5	6	7	8	9	10	11	12	13	14	15	16
	17	18	19	20	21	22	23	24	25	26	27	28	29	30	31	
August	1	2	3	4	5	6	7	8	9	10	11	12	13	14	15	16
	17	18	19	20	21	22	23	24	25	26	27	28	29	30	31	

Notes:

Mare Breeding Record

Horse's Name:		Registration #:
Breed:		**Age:**
Foal at Side: Y N		**Maiden:** Y N
Stallion Name		**Owned by:**
Breeding Method: Pasture Hand AI		**Semen:** Fresh Frozen
Breeding History:		

Code: N – no signs of heat   X – in heat   T – teased   B – bred   C – pregnancy check
P – pregnant   A – aborted   V – veterinary exam

Month																
January	1	2	3	4	5	6	7	8	9	10	11	12	13	14	15	16
	17	18	19	20	21	22	23	24	25	26	27	28	29	30	31	
February	1	2	3	4	5	6	7	8	9	10	11	12	13	14	15	16
	17	18	19	20	21	22	23	24	25	26	27	28	29			
March	1	2	3	4	5	6	7	8	9	10	11	12	13	14	15	16
	17	18	19	20	21	22	23	24	25	26	27	28	29	30	31	
April	1	2	3	4	5	6	7	8	9	10	11	12	13	14	15	16
	17	18	19	20	21	22	23	24	25	26	27	28	29	30		
May	1	2	3	4	5	6	7	8	9	10	11	12	13	14	15	16
	17	18	19	20	21	22	23	24	25	26	27	28	29	30	31	
June	1	2	3	4	5	6	7	8	9	10	11	12	13	14	15	16
	17	18	19	20	21	22	23	24	25	26	27	28	29	30		
July	1	2	3	4	5	6	7	8	9	10	11	12	13	14	15	16
	17	18	19	20	21	22	23	24	25	26	27	28	29	30	31	
August	1	2	3	4	5	6	7	8	9	10	11	12	13	14	15	16
	17	18	19	20	21	22	23	24	25	26	27	28	29	30	31	

Notes:

Mare Breeding Record

Horse's Name:	**Registration #:**
Breed:	**Age:**
Foal at Side: Y N	**Maiden:** Y N
Stallion Name:	**Owned by:**
Breeding Method: Pasture Hand AI	**Semen:** Fresh Frozen

Breeding History:

Code: N – no signs of heat   X – in heat   T – teased   B – bred   C – pregnancy check
P – pregnant   A – aborted   V – veterinary exam

January	1	2	3	4	5	6	7	8	9	10	11	12	13	14	15	16
	17	18	19	20	21	22	23	24	25	26	27	28	29	30	31	
February	1	2	3	4	5	6	7	8	9	10	11	12	13	14	15	16
	17	18	19	20	21	22	23	24	25	26	27	28	29			
March	1	2	3	4	5	6	7	8	9	10	11	12	13	14	15	16
	17	18	19	20	21	22	23	24	25	26	27	28	29	30	31	
April	1	2	3	4	5	6	7	8	9	10	11	12	13	14	15	16
	17	18	19	20	21	22	23	24	25	26	27	28	29	30		
May	1	2	3	4	5	6	7	8	9	10	11	12	13	14	15	16
	17	18	19	20	21	22	23	24	25	26	27	28	29	30	31	
June	1	2	3	4	5	6	7	8	9	10	11	12	13	14	15	16
	17	18	19	20	21	22	23	24	25	26	27	28	29	30		
July	1	2	3	4	5	6	7	8	9	10	11	12	13	14	15	16
	17	18	19	20	21	22	23	24	25	26	27	28	29	30	31	
August	1	2	3	4	5	6	7	8	9	10	11	12	13	14	15	16
	17	18	19	20	21	22	23	24	25	26	27	28	29	30	31	

Notes:

WEEKLY PLANNER

"Grooming: the process by which the dirt on
the horse is transferred to the groom"

DATE: _____

_____

_____

_____

_____

MONDAY
TUESDAY
WEDNESDAY
THURSDAY
FRIDAY
SATURDAY
SUNDAY

DATE: _____

_____

_____

_____

_____

MONDAY	
TUESDAY	
WEDNESDAY	
THURSDAY	
FRIDAY	
SATURDAY	
SUNDAY	

"It's always been and always will be the same in the world:
The horse does the work and the coachman is tipped."

DATE: _____

_____

_____

_____

_____

MONDAY
TUESDAY
WEDNESDAY
THURSDAY
FRIDAY
SATURDAY
SUNDAY

DATE: _____

_____

_____

_____

_____

MONDAY	
TUESDAY	
WEDNESDAY	
THURSDAY	
FRIDAY	
SATURDAY	
SUNDAY	

"The ass will carry his load, but not a double load; ride
not a free horse to death." - Miguel de Cervantes

DATE: _____

_____

_____

_____

_____

MONDAY

TUESDAY

WEDNESDAY

THURSDAY

FRIDAY

SATURDAY

SUNDAY

DATE: _____

_____

_____

_____

_____

MONDAY
TUESDAY
WEDNESDAY
THURSDAY
FRIDAY
SATURDAY
SUNDAY

"There is just as much horse sense as ever, but the horses have most of it."

DATE: _____

_____

_____

_____

_____

MONDAY
TUESDAY
WEDNESDAY
THURSDAY
FRIDAY
SATURDAY
SUNDAY

DATE: _____

_____

_____

_____

_____

MONDAY

TUESDAY

WEDNESDAY

THURSDAY

FRIDAY

SATURDAY

SUNDAY

"Riding a horse is not a gentle hobby, to be picked up and laid down
like a game of Solitaire. It is a grand passion." - Ralph Waldo Emerson

DATE: _____

_____

_____

_____

_____

MONDAY
TUESDAY
WEDNESDAY
THURSDAY
FRIDAY
SATURDAY
SUNDAY

DATE: _____

_____

_____

_____

_____

MONDAY	
TUESDAY	
WEDNESDAY	
THURSDAY	
FRIDAY	
SATURDAY	
SUNDAY	

"If your horse says no, you either asked the wrong
question, or asked the question wrong." - Pat Parelli

DATE: _____

_____

_____

_____

_____

| **MONDAY** |
| **TUESDAY** |
| **WEDNESDAY** |
| **THURSDAY** |
| **FRIDAY** |
| **SATURDAY** |
| **SUNDAY** |

DATE: _____

_____

_____

_____

_____

MONDAY

TUESDAY

WEDNESDAY

THURSDAY

FRIDAY

SATURDAY

SUNDAY

"A Horseman should know neither fear, nor anger." - James Rarey

DATE: _____

_____

_____

_____

_____

| **MONDAY** |
| **TUESDAY** |
| **WEDNESDAY** |
| **THURSDAY** |
| **FRIDAY** |
| **SATURDAY** |
| **SUNDAY** |

DATE: _____

_____

_____

_____

_____

MONDAY	
TUESDAY	
WEDNESDAY	
THURSDAY	
FRIDAY	
SATURDAY	
SUNDAY	

"The daughter who won't lift a finger in the house is the same child who cycles madly off in the pouring rain to spend all morning mucking out a stable." - Samantha Armstrong

DATE: _____

_____

_____

_____

_____

MONDAY
TUESDAY
WEDNESDAY
THURSDAY
FRIDAY
SATURDAY
SUNDAY

DATE: _____

_____
_____
_____
_____

MONDAY	
TUESDAY	
WEDNESDAY	
THURSDAY	
FRIDAY	
SATURDAY	
SUNDAY	

"I've spent most of my life riding horses. The rest I've just wasted."

DATE: _____

_____

_____

_____

_____

MONDAY
TUESDAY
WEDNESDAY
THURSDAY
FRIDAY
SATURDAY
SUNDAY

DATE: _____

_____

_____

_____

_____

MONDAY	
TUESDAY	
WEDNESDAY	
THURSDAY	
FRIDAY	
SATURDAY	
SUNDAY	

"If you act like you've only got fifteen minutes, it'll take all day. Act like you've got all day and it'll take fifteen minutes." - Monty Roberts

DATE: _____

_____

_____

_____

_____

MONDAY
TUESDAY
WEDNESDAY
THURSDAY
FRIDAY
SATURDAY
SUNDAY

DATE: _____

_____

_____

_____

_____

MONDAY

TUESDAY

WEDNESDAY

THURSDAY

FRIDAY

SATURDAY

SUNDAY

"Whoever said a horse was dumb, was dumb." - Will Rogers

DATE: _____

_____

_____

_____

_____

MONDAY	
TUESDAY	
WEDNESDAY	
THURSDAY	
FRIDAY	
SATURDAY	
SUNDAY	

DATE: _____

_____

_____

_____

_____

MONDAY	
TUESDAY	
WEDNESDAY	
THURSDAY	
FRIDAY	
SATURDAY	
SUNDAY	

"One who believes that he has mastered the art of
horsemanship has not yet begun to understand the horse."

DATE: _____

_____

_____

_____

_____

MONDAY
TUESDAY
WEDNESDAY
THURSDAY
FRIDAY
SATURDAY
SUNDAY

DATE: _____

_____

_____

_____

_____

MONDAY	
TUESDAY	
WEDNESDAY	
THURSDAY	
FRIDAY	
SATURDAY	
SUNDAY	

"The horse you get off is not the same as the horse you got on. It is your job
as a rider to ensure that as often as possible, the change is for the better."

DATE: _____

_____

_____

_____

_____

MONDAY
TUESDAY
WEDNESDAY
THURSDAY
FRIDAY
SATURDAY
SUNDAY

DATE: _____

_____

_____

_____

_____

_____

MONDAY	
TUESDAY	
WEDNESDAY	
THURSDAY	
FRIDAY	
SATURDAY	
SUNDAY	

"If a horse becomes more beautiful in the course of his work, it is a sign that the training principles are correct." - Colonel Podhajsky

DATE: _____

_____

_____

_____

_____

MONDAY
TUESDAY
WEDNESDAY
THURSDAY
FRIDAY
SATURDAY
SUNDAY

DATE: _____

_____

_____

_____

_____

MONDAY

TUESDAY

WEDNESDAY

THURSDAY

FRIDAY

SATURDAY

SUNDAY

"There are only two emotions that belong in the saddle; one is
a sense of humor and the other is patience." - John Lyons

DATE: _____

_____

_____

_____

_____

MONDAY
TUESDAY
WEDNESDAY
THURSDAY
FRIDAY
SATURDAY
SUNDAY

DATE: _____

_____

_____

_____

_____

MONDAY	
TUESDAY	
WEDNESDAY	
THURSDAY	
FRIDAY	
SATURDAY	
SUNDAY	

"You cannot train a horse with shouts and expect it to obey a whisper. " - Dagobert D. Runes

DATE: _____

_____

_____

_____

_____

MONDAY	
TUESDAY	
WEDNESDAY	
THURSDAY	
FRIDAY	
SATURDAY	
SUNDAY	

DATE: _____

_____
_____
_____
_____

| **MONDAY** |
| **TUESDAY** |
| **WEDNESDAY** |
| **THURSDAY** |
| **FRIDAY** |
| **SATURDAY** |
| **SUNDAY** |

"Correction does much for the horse, but encouragement does more."

DATE: _____

_____
_____
_____
_____

MONDAY
TUESDAY
WEDNESDAY
THURSDAY
FRIDAY
SATURDAY
SUNDAY

DATE: _____

_____

_____

_____

_____

MONDAY
TUESDAY
WEDNESDAY
THURSDAY
FRIDAY
SATURDAY
SUNDAY

"Horse sense is the thing a horse has which keeps it from betting on people." – W.C. Fields

DATE: _____

_____

_____

_____

_____

MONDAY
TUESDAY
WEDNESDAY
THURSDAY
FRIDAY
SATURDAY
SUNDAY

DATE: _____

_____

_____

_____

_____

MONDAY
TUESDAY
WEDNESDAY
THURSDAY
FRIDAY
SATURDAY
SUNDAY

"When in doubt, ask a horse."

DATE: _____

_____

_____

_____

_____

MONDAY
TUESDAY
WEDNESDAY
THURSDAY
FRIDAY
SATURDAY
SUNDAY

DATE: _____

_____

_____

_____

_____

MONDAY
TUESDAY
WEDNESDAY
THURSDAY
FRIDAY
SATURDAY
SUNDAY

"In training horses, one trains himself." - Antoine De Pluvinet

DATE: _____

_____

_____

_____

_____

MONDAY
TUESDAY
WEDNESDAY
THURSDAY
FRIDAY
SATURDAY
SUNDAY

DATE: _____

_____

_____

_____

_____

MONDAY
TUESDAY
WEDNESDAY
THURSDAY
FRIDAY
SATURDAY
SUNDAY

"When riding my horse I no longer have my heart in my chest, but between my knees."

DATE: _____

_____

_____

_____

_____

MONDAY
TUESDAY
WEDNESDAY
THURSDAY
FRIDAY
SATURDAY
SUNDAY

DATE: _____

_____

_____

_____

_____

MONDAY
TUESDAY
WEDNESDAY
THURSDAY
FRIDAY
SATURDAY
SUNDAY

"A horse is like a violin, first it must be tuned, and when tuned it must be accurately played."

DATE: _____

_____

_____

_____

_____

MONDAY
TUESDAY
WEDNESDAY
THURSDAY
FRIDAY
SATURDAY
SUNDAY

DATE: _____

_____

_____

_____

_____

MONDAY	
TUESDAY	
WEDNESDAY	
THURSDAY	
FRIDAY	
SATURDAY	
SUNDAY	

"A stubborn horse walks behind you, an impatient horse walks
in front of you, but a noble companion walks beside you."

DATE: _____

_____

_____

_____

_____

MONDAY
TUESDAY
WEDNESDAY
THURSDAY
FRIDAY
SATURDAY
SUNDAY

DATE: _____

_____

_____

_____

_____

MONDAY

TUESDAY

WEDNESDAY

THURSDAY

FRIDAY

SATURDAY

SUNDAY

"A horse loves freedom, and the weariest old work horse will roll on the ground or break into a lumbering gallop when he is turned loose into the open." - Gerald Raferty

DATE: _____

_____

_____

_____

_____

MONDAY	
TUESDAY	
WEDNESDAY	
THURSDAY	
FRIDAY	
SATURDAY	
SUNDAY	

DATE: _____

_____

_____

_____

_____

MONDAY
TUESDAY
WEDNESDAY
THURSDAY
FRIDAY
SATURDAY
SUNDAY

"I whisper to my horse, but he never listens!"

DATE: _____

_____

_____

_____

_____

MONDAY
TUESDAY
WEDNESDAY
THURSDAY
FRIDAY
SATURDAY
SUNDAY

DATE: _____

_____

_____

_____

_____

MONDAY
TUESDAY
WEDNESDAY
THURSDAY
FRIDAY
SATURDAY
SUNDAY

"Of all creatures God made at the Creation, there is none more excellent,
or so much to be respected as a horse." - Bedouin Legend

DATE: _____

_____

_____

_____

_____

MONDAY	
TUESDAY	
WEDNESDAY	
THURSDAY	
FRIDAY	
SATURDAY	
SUNDAY	

DATE: _____

_____

_____

_____

_____

MONDAY	
TUESDAY	
WEDNESDAY	
THURSDAY	
FRIDAY	
SATURDAY	
SUNDAY	

"The hardest thing about learning to ride is the ground!"

NOTES

"When you're young and you fall off a horse,
you may break something. When you're
my age, you splatter."
ROY ROGERS

17442145R00166

Made in the USA
Lexington, KY
19 November 2018